Christmas Crafts to Make and Do

TOP THAT

Licensed exclusively to Top That Publishing Ltd
Tide Mill Way, Woodbridge, Suffolk, IP12 1AP, UK
www.topthatpublishing.com
Copyright 2016 Tide Mill Media
0 2 4 6 8 9 7 5 3 1
Manufactured in China

Shimmering Stars

These simple shimmering stars look great as Christmas decorations!

YOU WILL NEED:

- 5 large lolly sticks
- Tracing paper and pencil
- PVA glue
- Clothes pegs
- Paint
- Paintbrush
- Coloured glitter
- Bowl
- Ribbon (optional)

1 Trace the star template to build your star on. Place one lolly stick on the star, then apply a blob of glue on each end. Lay the second stick on, placing one end over the blob of glue.

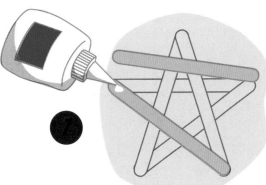

TEMPLATE

2 Apply a blob of glue on the second stick and carefully lay the third stick on, as shown.

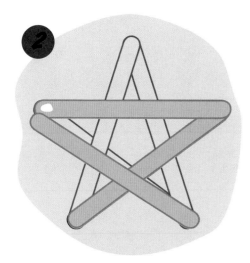

3 Now apply a blob of glue on the third stick and carefully lay the fourth stick on.

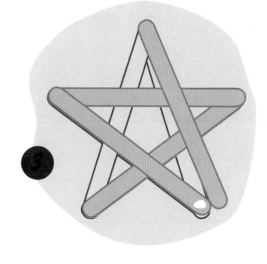

4 Repeat with the fifth stick. The best way to get your star to stick is to pinch each joint together with a clothes peg, as shown, and allow to dry.

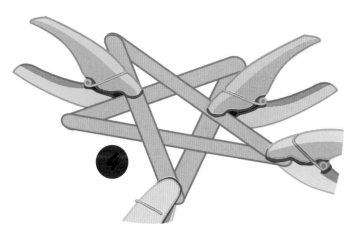

5 Once the glue is dry, remove the pegs and paint the star a colour which will match the glitter you want to use. Allow to dry.

6 When the paint is dry, coat the star with a thin layer of glue. Place in a bowl and carefully sprinkle with glitter, ensuring you cover it completely. Shake the loose glitter off and allow to dry.

7 When your star is dry it is ready to display. Why not tie a ribbon through one of the points to hang it.

Jolly Snowmen

You can let your imagination run wild when you decorate these cool snowmen!

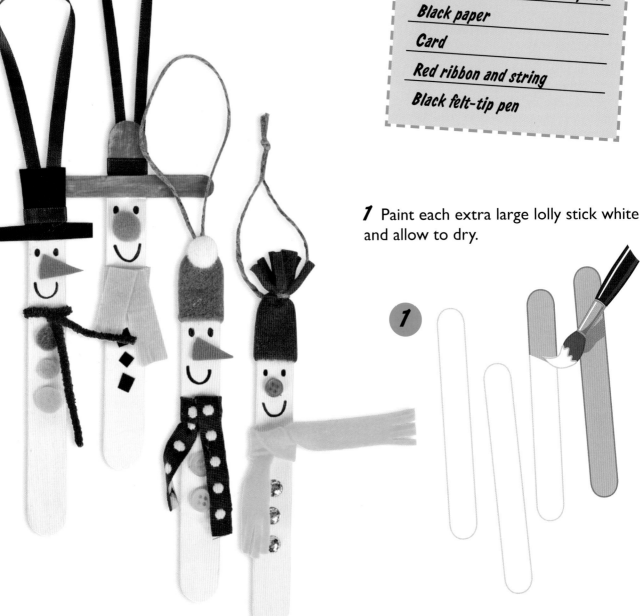

1 Paint each extra large lolly stick white and allow to dry.

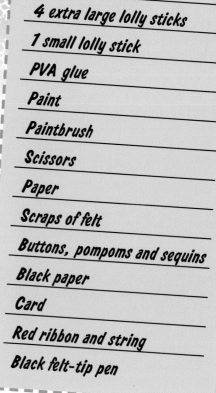

2 To make the snowman with the green hat, take the small lolly stick and glue it across one of the white lolly sticks, about 3 cm from one end, as shown. Let it dry and paint the hat shape green.

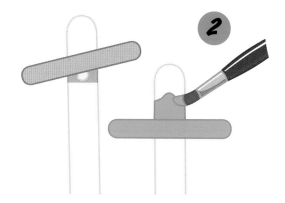

3 Out of a scrap of felt, cut the three shapes shown below to form a scarf. Snip the ends of the two smaller shapes to create a fringe.

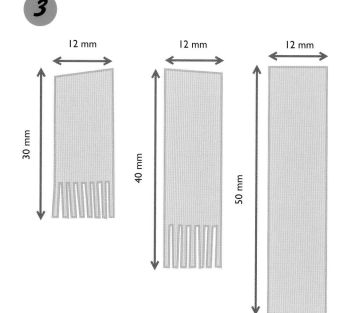

12 mm

12 mm

12 mm

30 mm

40 mm

50 mm

4 Wrap the large piece of felt around the neck of the snowman and glue. Position the other pieces at the angles shown, and glue.

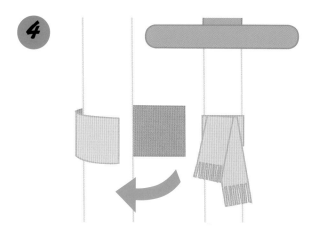

5 Finish decorating this snowman by sticking on a small orange pompom for his nose. Draw his face with a black felt-tip pen, and glue on tiny squares of black paper to make his buttons. Finally, tie red ribbon around his hat to decorate it and create a ribbon hanger.

6 For the red and blue hats, cut out felt in the sizes shown below. Snip the ends of the red felt to create a fringe.

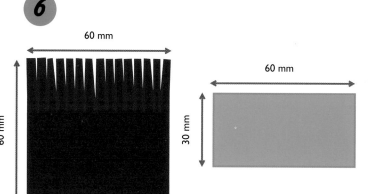

60 mm

60 mm

60 mm

30 mm

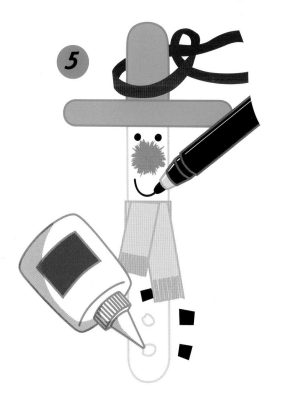

7 Add glue to the top of two sticks and wrap the felt around the tops, as shown. Fold the blue felt corners over to neaten. Leave to dry.

7

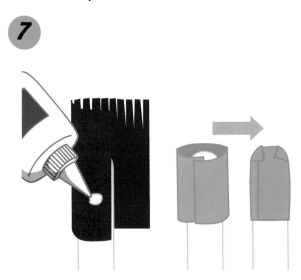

9 Make a top hat out of card and paint it black. Leave to dry.

9

Top Tip
Create more snowmen in different outfits and give them to your best friends!

8 Wrap string around the top of the red hat and pull tight, as shown, to form a hanger. Glue string to the back of the blue hat.

8

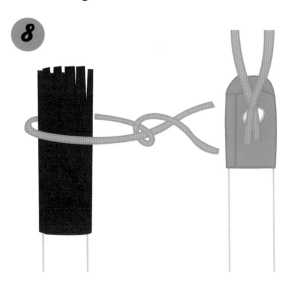

10 To finish your snowmen, create noses, scarves and buttons with ribbon, fuzzy sticks, scraps of felt, sequins or buttons. Draw on their faces with a black felt-tip pen. Let your imagination run wild!

10

Christmas Tree

If you're dreaming of a white Christmas, this tree is the perfect creative decoration.

YOU WILL NEED:

1 extra large lolly stick

2 large lolly sticks

2 medium lolly sticks

1 small lolly stick

PVA glue

Paint and a paintbrush

Silver card and silver ribbon

Scrap of card

Tracing paper and a pencil

Buttons, pompoms and sequins

1 Arrange your lolly sticks in the order shown below. Ask an adult to trim 1 cm from one medium stick and 1 cm from one large stick, keeping each end curved to match the uncut ends.

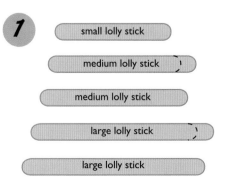

1 small lolly stick

medium lolly stick

medium lolly stick

large lolly stick

large lolly stick

2 Next, glue the sticks to the extra large lolly stick trunk, as shown, to make a Christmas tree shape.

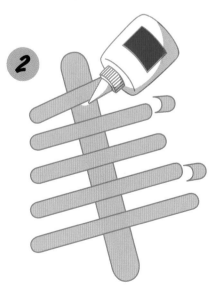

ADULT HELP NEEDED

3 Paint the tree green and allow it to dry.

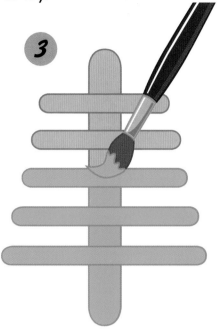

4 Wrap the silver ribbon around the tree and glue at the back, as shown.

5 Trace these star shapes and use them as templates to cut out stars from silver card. Set aside.

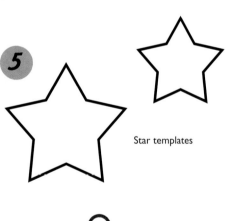

Star templates

6 Now cut out a piece of cardboard to the shape below to make the pot. Paint it red with white stripes.

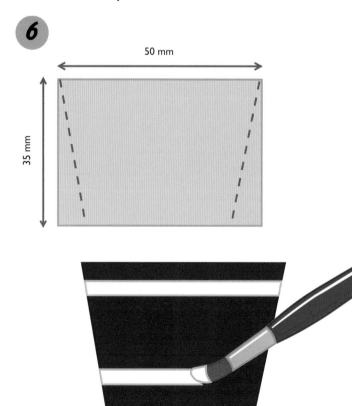

50 mm

35 mm

Top Tip
You could try using holographic card to make your stars. They'll shimmer and glimmer!

7 When the pot is dry, glue it to the base of the tree's trunk. Stick the silver stars in place, too.

8 Now you can put the finishing touches to your Christmas tree! Stick on pompoms, buttons, beads, sequins and glitter to make the most beautiful Christmas tree ever!

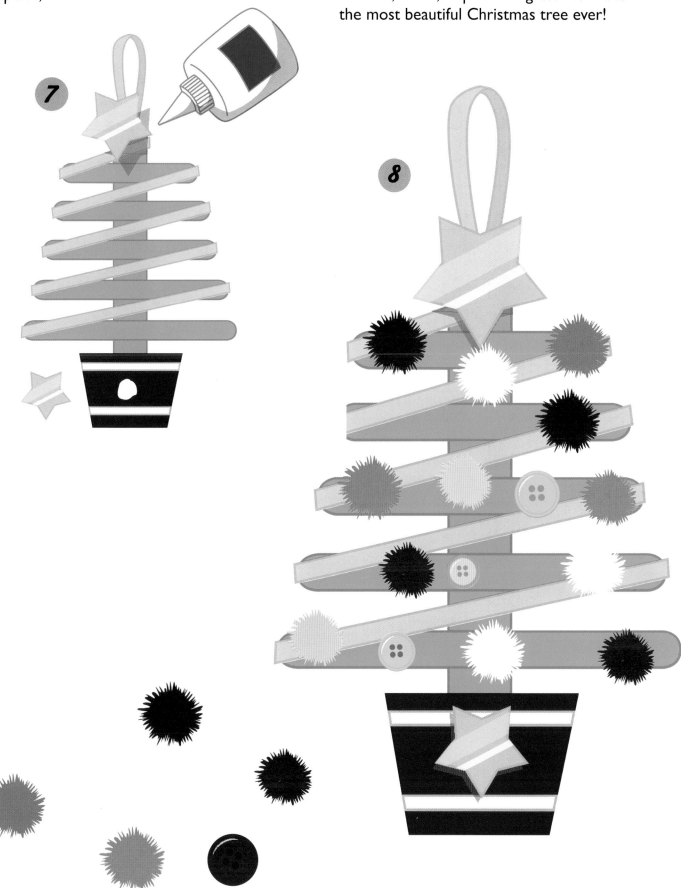

Pine Cone Owls

These little owls are the cutest decorations you can make with pine cones ... guaranteed!

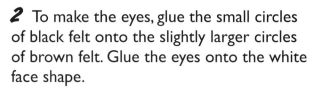

1 To make the owl with the large white face, cut out felt shapes, as shown.

2 To make the eyes, glue the small circles of black felt onto the slightly larger circles of brown felt. Glue the eyes onto the white face shape.

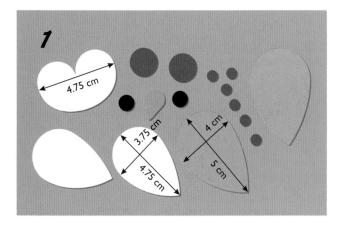

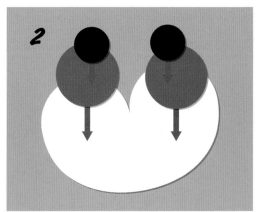

3 Glue the beak onto the face shape. Leave the face to dry.

4 To make the wings, glue the white wing shapes onto the slightly larger grey wing shapes. Make sure the top edges of the wings align. Add tiny brown circles on each wing for detail, as shown. Leave the wings to dry.

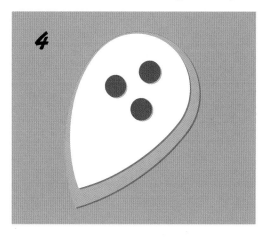

5 Once dry, glue the face and wings onto the pine cone, as shown. Leave to dry.

6 To make the feet, ask an adult to cut four 2.5 cm strips from the fuzzy stick. Bend the strips into 'U' shapes, then glue two strips together at right angles to make each foot. Leave to dry.

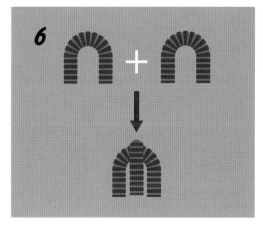

7 Glue your owl's feet at the front of the pine cone base. Once dry, they can be bent so your owl can perch anywhere!

Top Tip
Why not make a whole family! Experiment with different colours, tummy details and eyebrows to give your owls real character!

Festive Pompoms

WARNING!
When making mini pompoms, don't wrap the wool too tightly or you will cut off your circulation!

Mini pompoms are pretty just as they are, but they can be used to make some other great festive decorations, too (see pages 14 to 15).

1 Place the end of the wool around your fingers, as shown. For a small pompom, use two or three fingers. For a bigger pompom, use four fingers.

2 Wrap the wool around your fingers. The more you wrap, the fuller the pompom will be! When you have wrapped enough, cut the wool.

3 Cut a 30 cm length of wool and insert the end up between your fingers, as shown. You now have the piece of wool on one side of the pompom.

12

4 Place the other end of the wool through the tips of your fingers to hold in place, as shown, and tie the beginning of a knot. (You can do this on the palm side, if it's easier.)

5 Slide the wool off your fingers ...

6 ... then pull the knot tight. Tie another knot to make sure it is really secure.

7 Keeping the long pieces of wool out of the way, carefully slide your scissors into the loops and cut through the wool.

8 Your pompom should now look like this ...

9 ... so give it a light trim and fluff it up to look like this!

Pompom Room Decoration

Make this gorgeous room decoration to hang on your bedroom wall, across your mirror or your window.

Make lots of mini pompoms following the instructions on pages 12 to 13. Cut a length of wool to fit the place where you want to hang your decoration and fix it in place. Then, one at a time, tie the pompoms over the wool, adjusting the spacing until they look just right.

Top Tip
Pompoms make great Christmas tree decorations too!

Pompom Wreath

Make this cosy-looking wreath in any colours you like. It'll look amazing whatever you choose!

1 Place the large plate on the card and draw around it, then place the small plate in the middle and draw around that, too.

2 Ask an adult to help cut out the ring and make two small holes, as shown. Thread a doubled length of wool through the holes and tie the ends together.

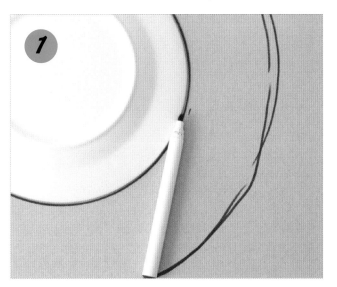

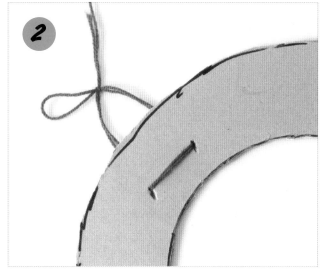

3 Now make lots of pompoms following the instructions on pages 12 to 13. Attach them with glue or double-sided sticky tape as you go. Tidy up any loose ends, then hang your decoration for a warm welcome!

Top Tip
We've used bright colours for our wreath, but pastel shades would look great too!

15

Christmas Candle Cookies

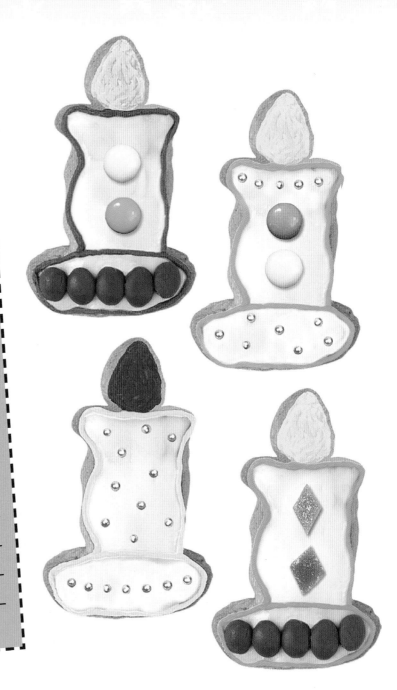

ADULT HELP NEEDED

These festive candles look great decorated with silver balls and sweets!

INGREDIENTS YOU WILL NEED:

120 g (4 oz) butter, softened

120 g (4 oz) sugar

½ teaspoon lemon juice

1 pinch cinnamon

1 pinch ground cloves

1 pinch nutmeg

230 g (8 oz) plain flour

100 g (3 ½ oz) hazelnuts, ground

Silver balls and sweets

Icing ingredients (opposite)

EQUIPMENT YOU WILL NEED:

Mixing bowl

Wooden spoon

Greaseproof paper

Rolling pin

Candle-shaped cookie cutter (or a knife)

Baking tray

Spatula

Wire rack

Sieve

Icing syringe

1 Preheat the oven to 200°C / 400°F / gas mark 6. Mix the butter, sugar, lemon juice, cinnamon, ground cloves, nutmeg, flour and hazelnuts together in a mixing bowl with a wooden spoon until a smooth dough is made.

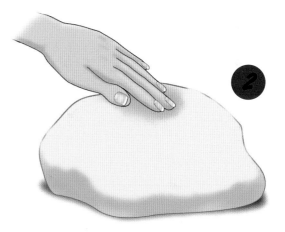

2 Place the mixture on top of a sheet of greaseproof paper, then put another sheet on top. Using a rolling pin, roll the dough flat between the sheets until it is 6 mm thick.

3 Using a candle-shaped cookie cutter or a sharp knife, cut out cookies from the dough. Place them onto a baking tray lined with greaseproof paper.

4 Bake the cookies for 12 minutes, or until they are golden brown. Ask an adult to take the hot tray from the oven. Use a spatula to transfer the cookies to a wire rack to cool.

5 Why not ice your cookies with a delicious water icing (see below). You could add piped detail with an icing syringe, then decorate with pretty silver balls and sweets!

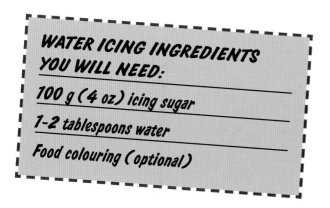

WATER ICING INGREDIENTS YOU WILL NEED:

100 g (4 oz) icing sugar

1-2 tablespoons water

Food colouring (optional)

Water Icing

Sift the icing sugar into a bowl and add enough water to make a thick smooth paste, using a wooden spoon. For coloured icing, add one or two drops of food colouring. You can add flavouring too, such as lemon or chocolate.

More Ideas

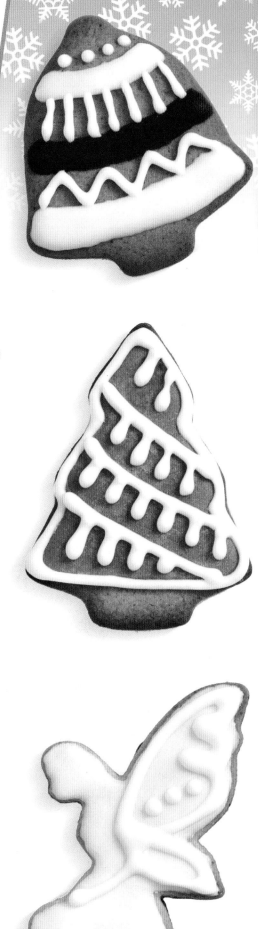

Once you have made the yummy Christmas Candle Cookies on pages 16 to 17, you could try out these fun festive designs.

Here are some ideas to get you started. Just follow the basic cooking instructions you have learnt and use icing in a piping bag or syringe to decorate.

Christmas Scratch Art

YOU WILL NEED:

Some stiff card

A pair of scissors

Colouring crayons

Black wax crayon

Ballpoint pen (lid on)

Make your own colourful Christmas cards and gift tags by creating this festive scratch art card. Then choose a design from pages 20 to 31 and recreate it by looking closely at each square on the grid and drawing what you see in each one.

1 Cut out a piece of card the size you want your picture to be. Then colour the card all over with a selection of colours to create a rainbow pattern.

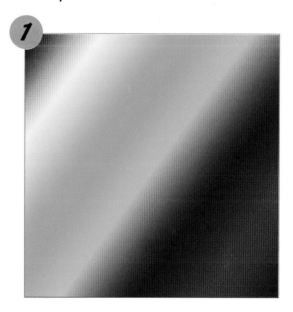

2 Now colour over the rainbow pattern with the black wax crayon.

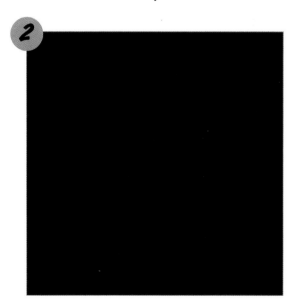

3 Scratch your picture onto the black outer coating using the ballpoint pen with its lid on. The colours underneath will show through!

19

DRAWING TEMPLATES

Copy the pictures square by square!

Jingle Bells

Christmas Tree

DRAWING TEMPLATES

Snowflake

Starry Night

DRAWING TEMPLATES

Copy the pictures square by square!

Stocking

Reindeer Face

DRAWING TEMPLATES

Presents

Santa's Sleigh

DRAWING TEMPLATES

Copy the pictures square by square!

Festive Wreath

Mistletoe

DRAWING TEMPLATES

Carol Singer

Angel

DRAWING TEMPLATES

Cracker!

Copy the pictures square by square!

Busy Elf

DRAWING TEMPLATES

Sledge

Party Fun

DRAWING TEMPLATES

Father Christmas

Copy the pictures square by square!

Jumping Reindeer

DRAWING TEMPLATES

Holly

Robin

DRAWING TEMPLATES

Surprise Gift

Copy the pictures square by square!

Smiling Elf

DRAWING TEMPLATES

Mr Snowman

Mrs Snowman

Snowball Cakes

These snowballs are much too tasty for throwing!

1 Preheat the oven to 170°C / 325°F / gas mark 3. With a wooden spoon or electric whisk, mix the icing sugar, butter and vanilla essence together in a mixing bowl until you have a smooth paste.

ADULT HELP NEEDED

INGREDIENTS YOU WILL NEED:

75 g (2 ½ oz) icing sugar

225 g (8 oz) butter, softened

2 teaspoons vanilla essence

250 g (9 oz) plain flour

90 g (3 oz) nuts, pecans or almonds finely chopped

½ teaspoon salt

TO DECORATE:

Icing sugar

EQUIPMENT YOU WILL NEED:

Wooden spoon or electric whisk

Mixing bowl

Sieve

Teaspoon

Baking tray

Greaseproof paper

Wire rack

Paper cases

2 Add the flour, nuts and salt to the mixture and stir. Keep mixing until all the ingredients are combined and you have a smooth dough.

3 Using a teaspoon, spoon small dollops of the dough onto a baking tray lined with greaseproof paper.

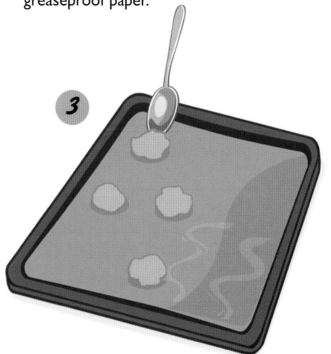

4 Bake the Snowball Cakes for 15 to 20 minutes. They should be just golden, so make sure you don't overcook them!

5 Ask an adult to remove the hot tray from the oven. Roll the Snowball Cakes across a plate of icing sugar before they cool completely.

6 Leave the decorated Snowball Cakes on a wire rack to cool. Serve them in paper cases with an extra dusting of icing sugar for a really snowy finish!

Top Tip

In step 3, either flatten the dough slightly to make the cakes on page 32, or roll it into balls like the cakes on the right.

Sparkly Glitter Balls

Create your own glitter balls for a truly sparkling Christmas. How many different designs will you make?

1 With newspaper protecting your work surface, cover the outsides of the two half balls with glue and sprinkle them both with glitter of your choice. Shake off any excess and allow to dry.

2 Dab spots of glue on the outside of the two halves, on top of the glitter. Place a star sequin on each spot. Fold a 20 cm length of gold thread and glue it to the flat side of one half ball. Glue the other half ball on top. Finish with a bow if you like, as shown above.

Wishing Bauble

YOU WILL NEED:

2 half polystyrene balls

Newspaper

PVA glue and spatula

Glitter in different colours

Gold thread

Notepaper

Scissors

Pen

Ribbon

Transform a glitter ball into a wishing bauble by adding a surprise inside ... a special Christmas wish!

1 With newspaper protecting your work surface, apply glue to the outside of both halves of the ball. Sprinkle them with glitter of your choice, decorate and allow to dry.

2 For a hanging loop, fold a 20 cm length of gold thread in half. Stick it to the flat side of one of the half balls, holding it in position while it dries.

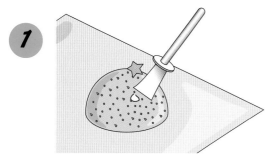

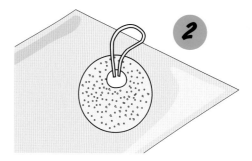

3 Cut a 2 x 10 cm strip of notepaper and write your Christmas wish on it. Fold it up in a zigzag, then glue it to the two halves of the ball, as shown.

4 Finish with ribbon, tied around your bauble to hold the two halves together. Secure with a bow.

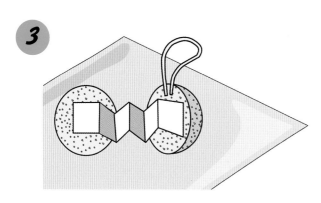

35

Peppermint Creams

Make these icy cool mints to enjoy after Christmas dinner.

INGREDIENTS YOU WILL NEED:

450 g (1 lb) icing sugar

1 egg white

Few drops of peppermint essence

Food colouring (optional)

EQUIPMENT YOU WILL NEED:

Sieve

Mixing bowl

3 or 4 small bowls

Whisk

Wooden spoon

Wire rack

1 Use the sieve to sift the icing sugar into the mixing bowl.

2 In a small bowl, whisk the egg white until frothy, then add to the icing sugar with a few drops of peppermint essence. Mix to a very thick paste with the wooden spoon.

4 Knead each batch of paste with your hands until very smooth. Pinch off small pieces and roll into balls, then flatten them into discs and place on the wire rack to set.

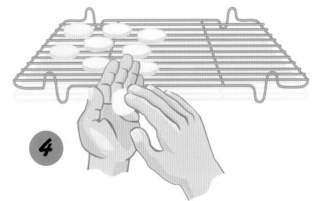

3 For coloured peppermint creams, put some of the paste in a small bowl, add a few drops of food colouring and mix well.

Christmas Crackers

Make your Christmas party table look extra festive with these glitzy crackers.

YOU WILL NEED:

Gold tissue paper

PVA glue and spatula

Card

Silver ribbon or tinsel

Glitter and sparkly decorations

Scissors

Christmas wishes written on notepaper and folded up small

1 Cut a 5 x 10 cm strip of card, roll up into a tube and secure with glue. (Wrapping the strip of card around a pen or pencil will help it to bend.)

2 Cut a 13 x 10 cm strip from gold-coloured tissue paper. At the edge of the 13 cm side, place the card tube centrally and secure with glue. Allow to dry. Before rolling the cracker's inner tube, tuck a Christmas wish inside.

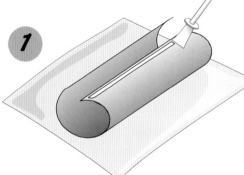

3 Roll the inner tube until all the tissue paper strip has been used. Secure with glue. Twist the excess tissue paper at either end.

4 Finish with ribbon or tinsel. Add a sparkly decoration to the top of your cracker, perhaps a piece of holly or a snowflake. Add glitter around the ends, as shown.

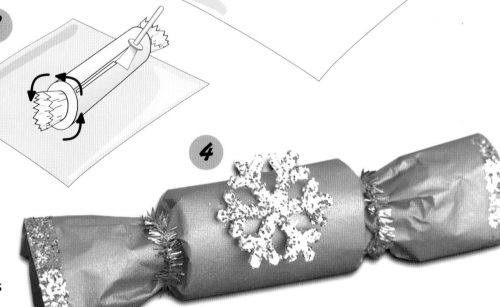

Cookie Tree Decorations

ADULT HELP NEEDED

These clever cookies will make your Christmas tree look really special.

INGREDIENTS YOU WILL NEED:

225 g (8 oz) plain flour

½ teaspoon ground mixed spice

100 g (4 oz) butter

100 g (4 oz) caster sugar

1 tablespoon milk

10 coloured boiled sweets

EQUIPMENT YOU WILL NEED:

Baking tray

Paper towel

Greaseproof paper

Sieve

Mixing bowl

Knife

Cling film

Rolling pin

Christmas-themed cookie cutters

Small plastic bag

Skewer

Wire rack

Ribbon or thread (for hanging cookies)

1 Preheat the oven to 180°C / 350°F / gas mark 4. Use a paper towel to grease the baking tray with a little butter. Sift the flour and ground mixed spice into a bowl.

2 Cut the butter into small pieces. Add it to the flour, and rub the mixture through your fingertips until it looks crumbly.

3 Add the sugar and milk to the bowl, and knead the mixture into a soft dough. Wrap the dough in cling film and put it in the fridge for 15 minutes.

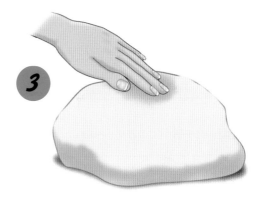

4 Put the dough onto a floured surface and roll it out. Use cookie cutters to cut out different shapes, and put them on the baking tray.

5 Put the boiled sweets in a plastic bag and crush them with a rolling pin. Carefully cut out a small hole from the centre of each cookie. Fill the holes with the crushed sweets. Use the skewer to pierce a hole in the top of each cookie.

6 Bake the cookies for 10–15 minutes, until they are golden brown and the sweets have melted. Once the melted sweets have set, carefully lift the cookies onto a wire rack to cool.

7 Thread the hole at the top of each cookie with ribbon or thread, and hang them on your Christmas tree!

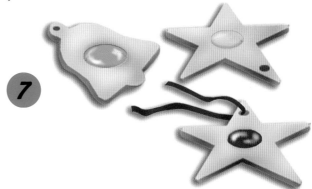

Candy Cane Tree Decorations

These cool candy canes look great hanging on the Christmas tree or in a glass for the festive table!

**INGREDIENTS
YOU WILL NEED:**

200 g (7 oz) butter

150 g (5 oz) caster sugar

2 teaspoons vanilla extract

1 egg

300 g (10 oz) plain flour, sifted

Red food colouring

**EQUIPMENT
YOU WILL NEED:**

Mixing bowl

Electric whisk

Cling film

Rolling pin

Knife

Baking tray

Baking parchment

Spatula

Wire rack

1 Preheat the oven to 180°C / 350°F / gas mark 4. Whisk the butter and sugar in a bowl, beat in the vanilla extract and the egg, and then add the flour. Beat until smooth, and separate the mixture into two.

2 Blend one half of the mixture with red food colouring, adding drops until you get the depth of colour you want. Wrap both mixtures in cling film and place them in the refrigerator to chill for 30 minutes.

3 Roll both of the doughs out until they are 5 mm thick. Ask an adult to cut the dough into 5 mm strips and chill for 5–10 minutes until slightly firm.

4 Take a strip of each colour, and press one on top of the other. Twist the strips together to make a candy cane plait, pinching the ends and bending them over as shown opposite. Repeat until all of the strips have been used.

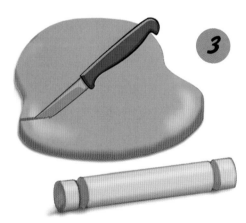

5 Place onto a baking tray lined with baking parchment. Chill for 10 minutes, and then put them in the oven to bake for 8 minutes. Use a spatula to transfer the candy canes onto a wire rack to cool.

Top Tip
Instead of red food colouring, you could use blue or green for a candy cane twist!

Finger Puppets

Before you begin to make your puppets, you will need to cut out a paper pattern for each part and collect all of the items in the list at the beginning.

Use the templates at the end of each project to make paper patterns. Draw, or trace, all your shapes onto thin paper, lay them on the felt, pin them to stop them moving, then cut around the shapes.

To make the main body of each puppet, you need to cut two identical body shapes – one for the front and one for the back. Make two paper patterns of the shape, pin them onto the felt, then cut them out.

If you are using a tube of glue, hold it as you would a pencil, then draw a narrow line of glue around the edge of one body shape. Do not glue the base edge. Press the second body shape on top. The legs, face, tummy, arms and so on are added in layers onto the body and stuck into place.

Father Christmas

Make this Father Christmas finger puppet so he can deliver presents to good girls and boys.

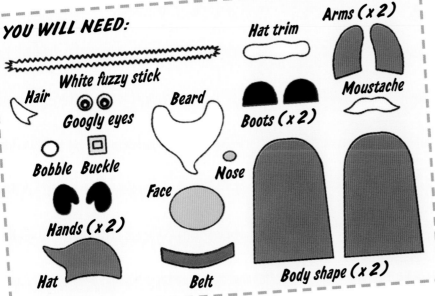

YOU WILL NEED:

White fuzzy stick

Hair

Googly eyes

Bobble Buckle

Hands (x 2)

Hat

Beard

Face

Belt

Nose

Hat trim

Boots (x 2)

Arms (x 2)

Moustache

Body shape (x 2)

1 Cut out all the pieces from the felt (see templates on page 44). On one body shape, use glue to draw a line around the edges, but not on the base edge. Press the other body onto the glued body.

1

2

2 Glue the boots, belt and buckle onto the body, as shown. Glue the right hand to the edge of the belt, so the wrist sticks out over the body edge.

3 Assemble the left and right arms and attach to the body, as shown. Glue the face to the body and add the hair, at an angle.

4 Glue the hat and the beard into place, as shown. Fix the moustache to the face with the ends overlapping the beard. Fix the eyes so that they overlap the moustache.

Templates

5 Cut two bits of white fuzzy stick to glue over the wrists. Glue the hat trim to the hat's edge. Glue the nose to the centre of the moustache and the bobble to the hat.

Harry Reindeer

Harry the reindeer wants to help
Father Christmas deliver presents.

YOU WILL NEED:

Brown fuzzy stick

Hooves (x 4)

Inner ear (x 2)

Googly eyes

Highlight

Nose

Head (x 2)

Outer ear piece

Legs (x 2)

Body shape (x 2)

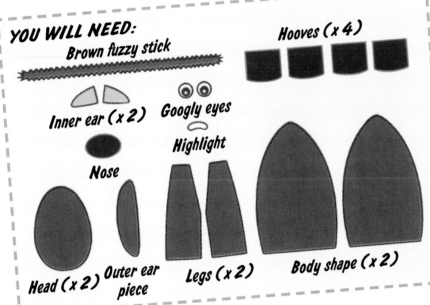

1 Cut out all the felt pieces. On one body shape, use glue to draw a line around the curved edges, but not on the base edge. Press the other body shape onto the glued body.

1

2

2 Glue a black hoof to each corner of the base edge. Centre the outer ear piece at the top of the body and glue in place.

3 Cut pieces of fuzzy stick and twist together to make antler shapes, as shown. Centre on the outer ear piece and glue in place. Add the inner ears to each side.

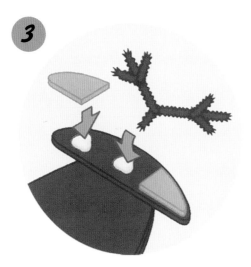

4 Glue a hoof to the widest end of each leg piece. Line up the legs with the straight edge of the outer ear piece, and glue to the body as shown – but don't glue the whole leg down.

5 Glue the face over the join in the antlers and over the tops of the legs. Add the nose and eyes, and glue the highlight in place.

Templates

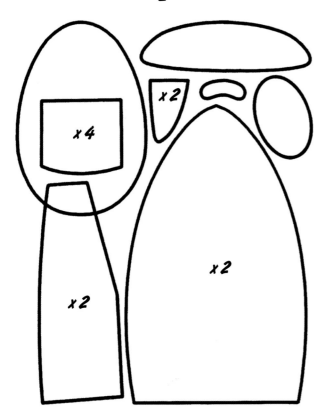

x4

x2

x2

x2

Eddie Elf

Is Eddie busy helping Father Christmas prepare the presents or is he chatting to the reindeer?

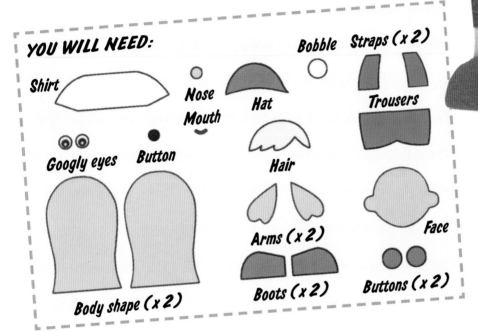

YOU WILL NEED:

Shirt

Nose
Mouth

Hat

Bobble   Straps (x 2)

Trousers

Googly eyes   Button

Hair

Body shape (x 2)

Arms (x 2)

Boots (x 2)

Face

Buttons (x 2)

---

1 Cut out all the felt pieces. On one body shape, use glue to draw a line around the edges, but not on the base edge. Press the other body shape to the glued body.

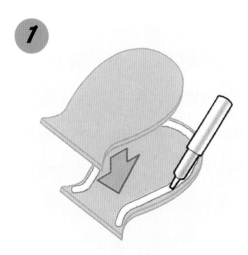

1

2

2 Glue the boots to the bottom edge. Centre the shirt across the body. Stick a hand to each end of the shirt and glue them all together, as shown.

3 Glue the trousers to the body, as shown. Fix the straps into place and add a button over each one where it meets the trouser top.

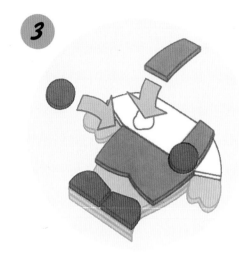

4 Glue the face into place, as shown. Attach the hair to the upper head, then glue the hat to the head, over the hair.

Templates

5 Glue the bobble to the right side of the hat and glue on the eyes. Fix the nose and the mouth in place to finish Eddie.

More Ideas

Once you have made the festive finger puppets on pages 43 to 48, you could design some more of your own.

Here are some ideas to get you started. Just follow the basic construction techniques you have learnt to put all the separate pieces together.

Star Friendship Bracelet

Make this twinkling friendship bracelet to say 'Happy Christmas' to a best friend. Or make it for yourself and wear it on Christmas Day!

YOU WILL NEED:

Sticky tape

Clipboard or thick card

Scissors

1 lilac thread, *28 cm long*

1 pale blue thread, *28 cm long*

2 dark blue threads *28 cm long*

4 white star beads

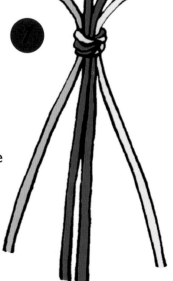

1 Knot the four threads together at one end. Use a piece of sticky tape to attach the knotted end to the top of the clipboard or card, then separate the threads as shown.

2 Take the pale blue thread over the dark blue threads, then pass it underneath the dark blue threads and return it to its original position.

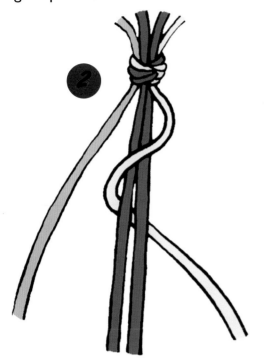

3 Now take the lilac thread and do exactly the same. You'll see that you have made a cross pattern with the two different colours.

4 Repeat steps 2 and 3 for about 2 cm, then thread one of the star beads onto the dark blue threads.

5 Repeat steps 2–4 three more times, finishing the bracelet with 2 cm of cross pattern and a knot to tie the loose ends together.

Top Tip
If you can't find star beads, look for something in gold or silver for a festive shine.

Christmas Fairy

ADULT
HELP
NEEDED

Make this pretty fairy and use her as a festive room decoration, or as a magical addition to the top of your Christmas tree.

YOU WILL NEED:

Dolly peg

Black felt-tip pen

½ pink fuzzy stick

PVA glue

1 m of yellow thread

Scissors

Lilac tissue paper, 30 x 30 cm

Purple tissue paper, 30 x 30 cm

1 m of gold thread

Purple tinsel trim

Sequins

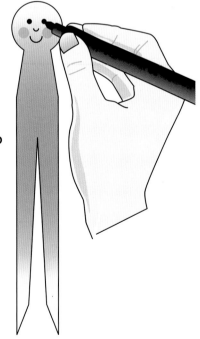

1 Use the felt-tip pens to draw on the dolly peg's features.

2 Take half a pink fuzzy stick. Bend over the ends to make the fairy's arms and hands. Stick it to the back of the dolly peg and leave it to dry.

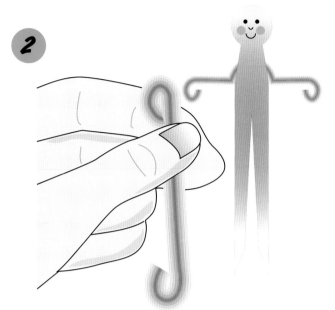

3 Take the yellow thread. Fold it over and repeat until you have the desired length of hair, then stick to the dolly peg's head. Trim the ends with scissors to neaten when dry.

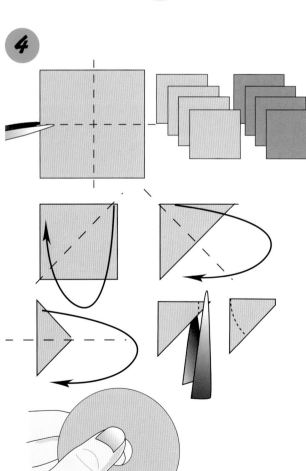

4 Take a sheet of lilac tissue paper and a sheet of purple tissue paper and cut them into four equal squares, as shown. Take one square and fold it into a triangle. Fold it again and then once more, as shown. Snip off the right-hand point, then cut out the shape shown. Unfold the tissue to reveal a layer of the fairy's skirt. Repeat with another lilac tissue square and then with two purple tissue squares.

5 Cut out a piece from one of the purple rings, as shown.

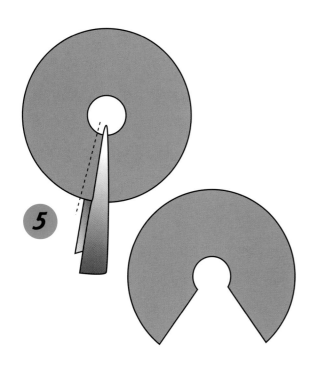

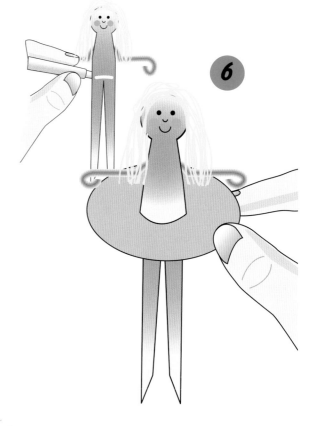

6 Spread a small ring of glue around your dolly's waist, then stick the lilac tissue rings in place to make the underskirt.

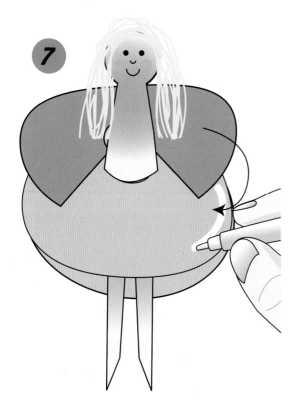

Top Tip
Try separating the hair to give your fairy bunches, like the fairy on page 52. You could make her a wand too, when you've finished!

7 Stick the purple piece of tissue paper on top of the underskirt, leaving a gap, as shown.

8 Fold a square of lilac tissue paper in half. Cut it according to the pattern below. Unfold it and slip it over the fairy's head. Stick the sides together to make her top (right).

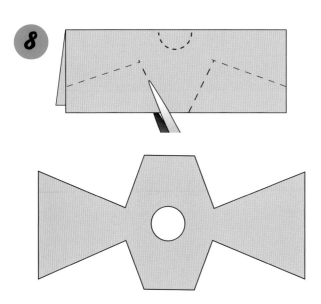

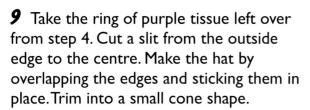

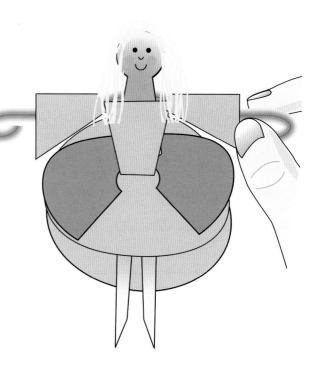

9 Take the ring of purple tissue left over from step 4. Cut a slit from the outside edge to the centre. Make the hat by overlapping the edges and sticking them in place. Trim into a small cone shape.

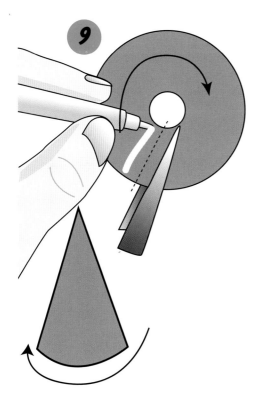

10 Stick the hat on to the fairy's head, then decorate her outfit. Use gold thread around her waist and on the top of her hat, and purple tinsel trim around her skirt. Use sequins to add sparkle, and any offcuts of tinsel trim for her shoes.

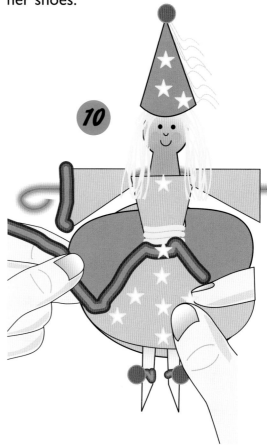

Christmas Party Cakes

ADULT
HELP
NEEDED

Use lots of brightly-coloured icing to decorate these fun party cakes!

INGREDIENTS YOU WILL NEED:

225 g (8 oz) self-raising flour

75 g (3 oz) margarine

75 g (3 oz) caster sugar

1 egg

75-100 ml (3-4 fl. oz) milk

EQUIPMENT YOU WILL NEED:

Paper cases

Bun tin

Mixing bowl

Sieve

Spoon

Wire rack

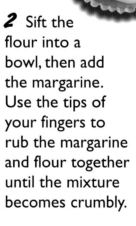

2 Sift the flour into a bowl, then add the margarine. Use the tips of your fingers to rub the margarine and flour together until the mixture becomes crumbly.

3 Add the sugar and mix it in. Now stir in the egg. Finally, add enough milk to make the mixture creamy.

4 Put spoonfuls of the mixture into the paper cases. Bake the cakes for 10–15 minutes, until they are golden brown, then leave them to cool on a wire rack.

1 Preheat the oven to 200°C / 400°F / gas mark 6. Put the paper cases in the bun tin.

Decorating Your Cakes

INGREDIENTS YOU WILL NEED:

100 g (4 oz) icing sugar

1 egg white

Food colouring

EQUIPMENT YOU WILL NEED:

Small bowl

Whisk

Mixing bowl

Sieve

Wooden spoon

Icing syringe

Now for the fun part ... the decoration!

You can decorate your cakes with water icing (see page 17), or follow the instructions below for making royal icing. Whichever method you use, go for lots of different colours, using an icing syringe to make patterns if you wish. Add a yummy selection of edible decorations to finish with.

Royal Icing

To make royal icing, beat an egg white in a small bowl. Sift the icing sugar into the bowl. Beat the mixture with a wooden spoon until the icing is smooth and thick. Add a drop of food colouring if you wish. Spoon the icing into an icing syringe and carefully pipe your decoration onto the cakes. Leave the icing until almost set, then finish with more decorations on top.

Variations

Chocolate Chip Party Cakes

Sift 25 g (1 oz) cocoa into the bowl with the flour. Mix in a handful of chocolate chips. When the cakes are cooked and cooled, cover them with chocolate water icing (see page 17).

Coconut Party Cakes

Add 50 g (2 oz) desiccated coconut to the mixture with the sugar. When the cakes are cooked, top them with lemon water icing (see page 17) and sprinkle them with more coconut.

Cherry Party Cakes

Add 100 g (4 oz) chopped glacé cherries to the mixture with the sugar. When the cakes are cooked, cover them with lemon water icing (see page 17) and top each cake with half a glacé cherry.

Make Your Own Nativity Scene

⚠ ADULT HELP NEEDED

Get ready to transform ordinary wooden dolly pegs into a beautiful nativity scene. Just follow the simple illustrated step-by-step instructions on pages 60 to 79 and use the templates supplied on pages 94 to 96.

Before You Start ...

To make the characters, you will need a collection of materials including dolly pegs, coloured felt and tissue paper, coloured thread, fuzzy sticks, pompoms, beads, buttons and sequins. You will also need some basic items including scissors, PVA glue and a felt-tip pen. Check the list at the beginning of each project and gather everything together before you start.

Get Creative!

The step-by-step instructions are a guide to making each character. If you don't have all the items listed, or if you want to dress the characters differently, go ahead and experiment with the designs and materials!

Follow these top tips to create perfect dolly peg characters every time!

⭐ Keep both hands free to decorate your dolly pegs by standing your pegs in a piece of sticky putty.

⭐ Allow the glue to dry in between steps, holding items in place with a paper clip. Your patience will make it easier to complete each stage!

⭐ Felt or tissue paper work well for clothes, but you could also try fabric scraps, coloured paper or even tinfoil.

⭐ Keep any offcuts of material to add shoes and accessories. Beads, sequins, buttons and scraps of ribbon are all great for decorating your characters.

⭐ Use your imagination to create accessories for your characters; we have used a golf tee and a walnut shell – see if you can spot them!

⭐ Give each character a different expression: calm, happy, joyful, surprised … you decide!

WARNING!
Fuzzy sticks and scissors have sharp points. Ask an adult to help you bend fuzzy sticks and with any steps that need scissors.

Joseph: page 63

Mary: page 60

Shepherd: page 67

Sheep: page 70

King: page 71

Baby Jesus: page 66

Angel: page 75

Camel: page 74

Mary

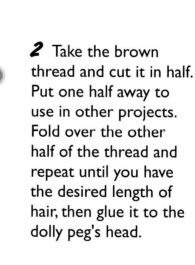

1 Take half a pink fuzzy stick. Bend over the ends to make the hands. Stick it to the back of the dolly peg to create the arms.

2 Take the brown thread and cut it in half. Put one half away to use in other projects. Fold over the other half of the thread and repeat until you have the desired length of hair, then glue it to the dolly peg's head.

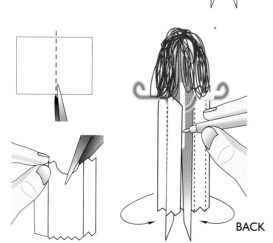

3 Cut the white felt in half. On one half, cut a small circle in the middle, as shown, then pleat the felt. Wrap it around the dolly peg and glue into place.

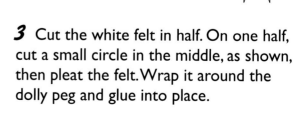

BACK

4 Take a length of blue ribbon, tie it around the waist and finish with a bow.

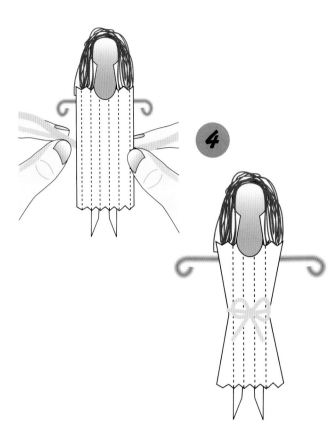

5 For the cloak you will need the light blue felt. Place Mary on the felt, short side at the top, then bend the edges over the fuzzy stick arms and glue. Hold in place while drying.

Top Tip
You can use a paper clip to hold the felt in place while the glue dries.

6 Put a dot of glue below the point you just made in step 5, and fold the felt over onto the dot. Repeat for both sides and hold in place while drying.

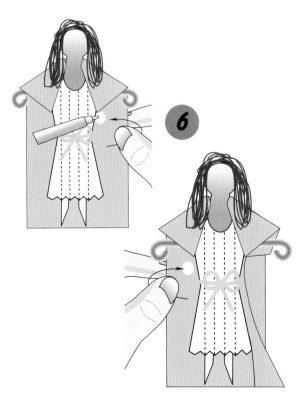

7 For the headdress, take the remaining piece of white felt and cut it in half. Put one piece away to use later. Glue the edge of the felt onto the centre of Mary's forehead. When dry, flip the felt piece over behind her head.

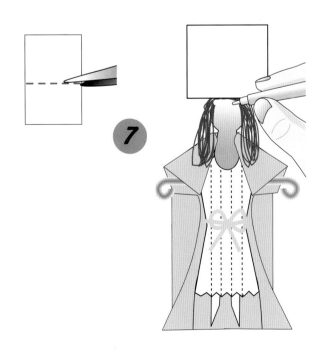

8 Take one corner of the headdress, as shown, bend it over and glue it in place. Repeat for both sides.

9 Turn the dolly peg over. Tuck under both corners of the headdress and secure with a dot of glue on each flap.

10 To finish Mary, use a black felt-tip pen to draw her features. Cut the loops in her hair to make individual strands.

Top Tip
You could add scraps of white felt for her cuffs.

Joseph

YOU WILL NEED:

Dolly peg

½ pink fuzzy stick

Light brown felt, 9 x 18 cm

1 m gold thread

Orange felt, 9 x 18 cm

Cloak template (page 96)

Tracing paper and pencil

White paper

1 m brown thread

Scissors

PVA glue

Black felt-tip pen

1 Take half a pink fuzzy stick. Bend over the ends to make the hands. Stick it to the back of the dolly peg to create the arms.

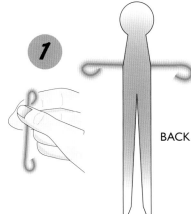

BACK

2 Cut the light brown felt in half. Put one half away to use later. Wrap the other half around the front of the dolly peg and then turn the peg over.

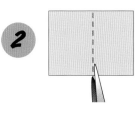

FRONT

3 Bend the edges over the fuzzy stick arms and glue, holding in place while drying.

BACK

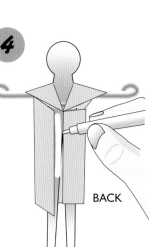

BACK

4 Spread glue down the back of the peg and secure the remaining felt.

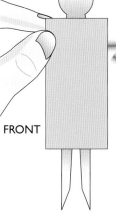

5 Take the length of gold thread and cut it in half. Put one half away for later projects. Cut the other half in half again and tie around the waist. Finish with a knot and hanging tails. Trim off the excess thread and wind it around the legs in a criss-cross pattern to make sandals. Glue in place at the top.

6 Fold the orange felt in half. Trace the cloak template (page 96) onto the white paper and cut out. Put the top of the cloak shape onto the folded edge of felt, draw around it and cut it out.

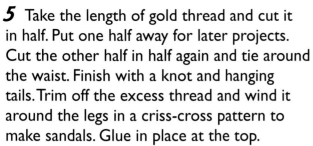

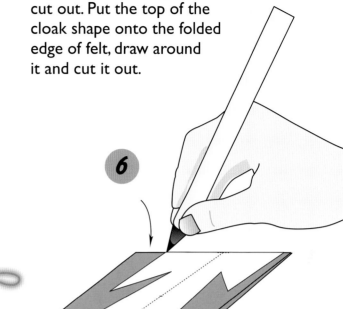

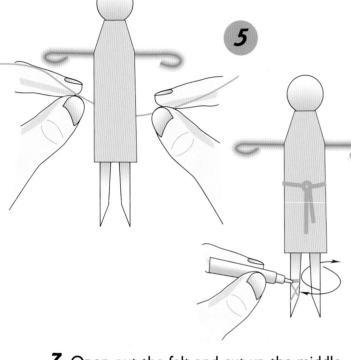

8 To create the pointed look for the cloak, just trim the ends at an angle with a pair of scissors.

7 Open out the felt and cut up the middle of one side. Make a little cut on each side along the crease, ready to create lapels. Gently place the cloak over the arms and glue the edges together. Fold back the lapels.

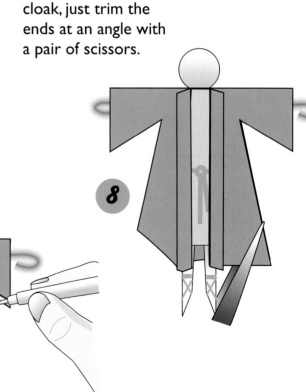

9 Cut the brown thread in half. Fold over one half and repeat until you have enough hair, then glue it to the head. Trim the ends of the hair and stick these pieces to the face for a beard.

10 To create the headdress, take the remaining piece of light brown felt and cut it in half. Glue the edge of one half to the centre of Joseph's forehead. Gently flip the felt behind his head and bend the top corners over to the front. Glue in place.

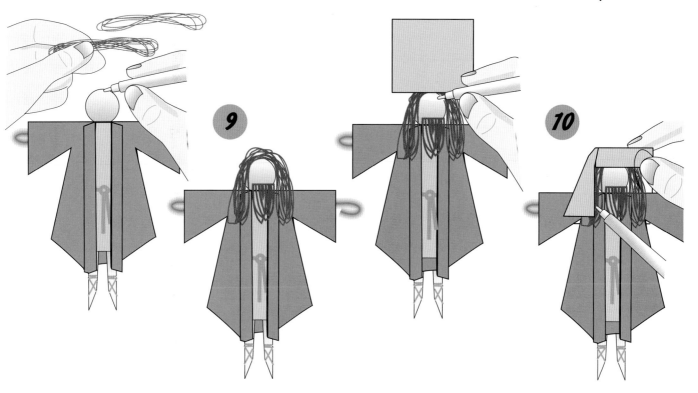

11 Turn over and secure both flaps, as shown, with a dot of glue. Then take the small piece of gold thread and tie around the head for a headband.

12 Finally, finish Joseph using a black felt-tip pen to draw his features.

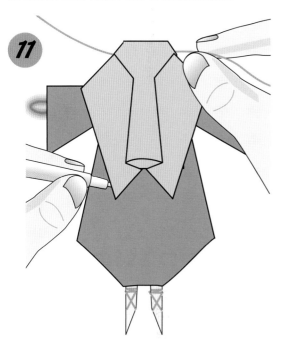

Baby Jesus

YOU WILL NEED:

1 wooden bead

Small rectangle of white felt

Crib template (page 96)

Tracing paper and pencil

Card

Coloured felt-tip pens

Yellow tissue paper

Scissors

PVA glue

Black felt-tip pen

1 Glue the bead onto a small rectangle of white felt near one long edge. Fold over the top.

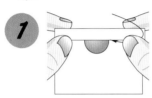

2 Then take a corner, fold over and secure in the centre with glue.

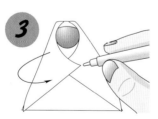

3 Repeat for the other side, overlapping the felt as shown.

4 Take one corner point and fold it up under the head and secure with glue. Repeat for the other side.

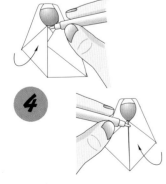

5 Using a black felt-tip pen, draw in the baby's face.

The Crib

We used half a walnut shell for the crib, but if you don't have one you can use the template supplied.

1 Trace the crib template (page 96) onto the card, then cut out. Use felt-tip pens to colour it like wood.

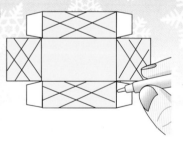

2 Spread glue on the tab edges, fold into a box shape, then secure the glued edges by tucking them inside the flaps.

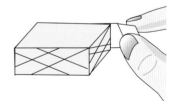

3 Cut up some yellow tissue paper for straw, or you could use wool, string or even pet hay. Fill the crib and place Jesus inside.

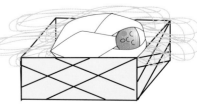

Shepherd

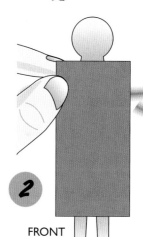

1 Take half a pink fuzzy stick. Bend over the ends to make the hands. Stick it to the back of the dolly peg to create the arms.

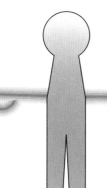

2 Cut the light brown felt in half. Save one half for later. Wrap the other half around the front of the dolly peg, then turn the peg over.

FRONT

3 Bend the edges over the fuzzy stick arms and glue, holding in place while drying. Spread glue down the back of the peg and secure the remaining felt.

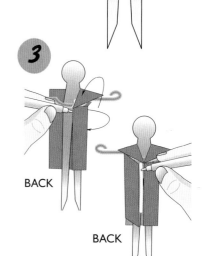

BACK

BACK

4 Fold the dark brown felt in half. Trace the cloak template (page 96) onto the white paper and cut out. Put the top of the cloak shape onto the folded edge of felt, draw around it and cut it out.

5 Open out the felt and cut up the middle of one side. Make a little cut on each side along the crease, ready to create lapels. Gently place the cloak over the arms and glue the edges together.

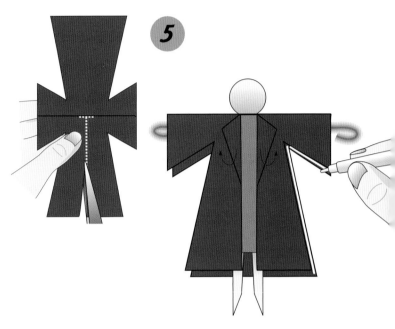

6 Take the black thread and cut it in half. Fold over one half and repeat until you have enough for a moustache, then glue it to the face. Trim the ends off and stick these pieces in the centre of the moustache, for a beard.

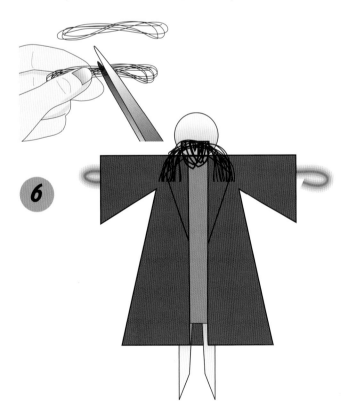

7 To create the headdress, take the remaining piece of light brown felt and cut it in half. Glue the edge of one half to the centre of the shepherd's forehead.

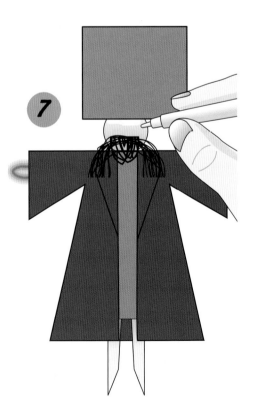

8 Gently flip the felt behind the head and bend the top corners over to the front. Glue in place, then tuck both ends behind the head.

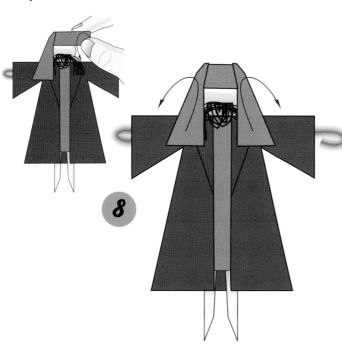

9 Turn over the dolly peg and bend both ends in under the headdress, as shown. Secure with glue.

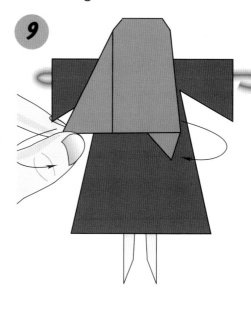

10 Take a piece of string, wrap it around the head, cross it over at the back and glue in place.

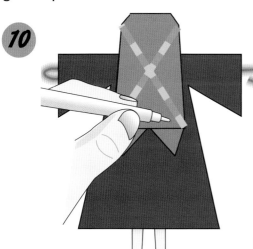

11 Wrap another piece of string around the waist and tie with a knot.

12 Use a black felt-tip pen to draw the shepherd's features. Finally, give him a crook by bending over the end of half a gold fuzzy stick, as shown. You could even add some sack material for an authentic look (see photograph on page 67)!

Sheep

YOU WILL NEED:

White chenille or thick wool

2 black pompoms

1 black fuzzy stick

Scissors

PVA glue

1 Take a long piece of white chenille and tie a loose knot at one end. Wind the rest of the chenille around the knot, over and over again, creating the sheep's body.

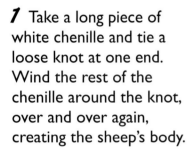

2 Glue the loose end underneath the body and leave to dry. Then glue one of the small black pompoms to the front, for the head.

3 Cut the black fuzzy stick in half, then cut both halves into three equal pieces.

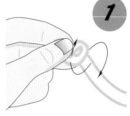

4 Bend over the ends of all the pieces, as shown.

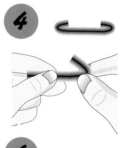

5 Glue one piece over the black pompom to create the sheep's ears.

6 Bend two pieces in half and glue them under the sheep for the legs.

7 Repeat steps 1 to 6 with more chenille and the remaining fuzzy stick pieces to create the second sheep.

King

YOU WILL NEED:

Dolly peg

½ brown fuzzy stick

Light purple felt, 9 x 18 cm

Gold sequins: small stars, small circles, a square

1 m gold thread

Cloak template (page 96)

Tracing paper and pencil

White paper

Dark purple felt, 9 x 18 cm

1 m black thread

1 big purple pompom

Purple tinsel thread, or similar

Scissors

PVA glue

Black felt-tip pen

1 Take half a brown fuzzy stick. Bend over the ends to make the hands. Stick it to the back of the dolly peg to create the arms.

2 Cut the light purple felt in half. Save one half for use later. Wrap the other half around the front of the dolly peg, then turn the peg over.

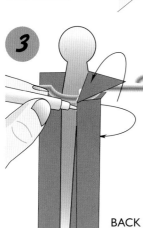

BACK

3 Bend the edges over the fuzzy stick arms and glue, holding in place while drying.

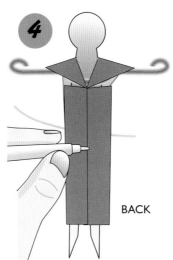

BACK

4 Spread glue down the back of the peg and secure the remaining felt. Take a small piece of gold thread and glue it around the waist for a belt.

5 Decorate the front of the tunic with star sequins and a gold square sequin for a buckle.

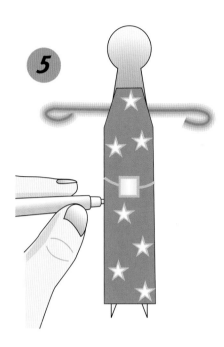

6 For the cloak, take the dark purple felt and follow step 6 on page 64. (Keep the offcuts for step 8.)

Open out the felt and cut up the middle of one side. Make a little cut on each side along the crease, and fold back to make lapels. Fold over the sleeve ends to create cuffs. Place the cloak over the arms and glue the edges together.

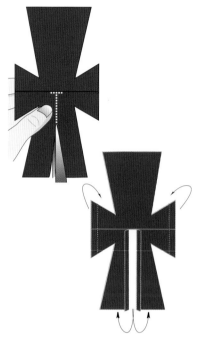

7 Take the black thread and cut it in half. Fold over one half and repeat until you have enough for a beard. Glue it to the face. Fold the other half over and glue onto the head for hair.

8 Glue the purple pompom on top of the head. Then cut two thin strips of light purple felt. Twist one strip and glue it around the neck to create a scarf. Twist the other strip and glue it below the pompom, like a hat brim.

9 Decorate the cloak by gluing lengths of tinsel thread down the front lapels and around the sleeves. Or you could use glitter glue instead!

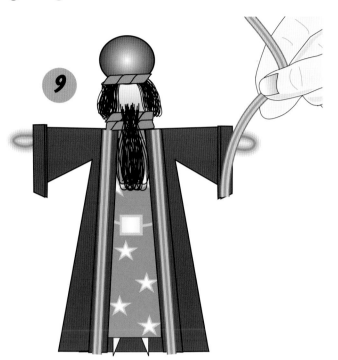

10 Glue square sequins on the bottom of each cuff and at the base of each lapel. Glue a large sequin in the middle of the pompom for a jewel.

11 Use a black felt-tip pen to draw the king's features. Snip the ends of his hair and beard to make individual strands.

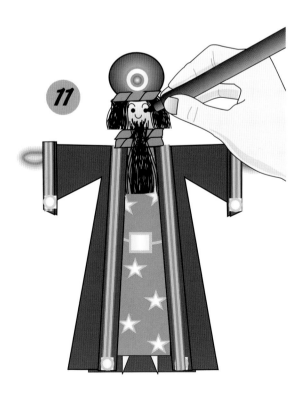

12 Finally, make a gift for your king to present to the baby Jesus. A scrunched-up gold sweetie paper or a bead work well – use your imagination!

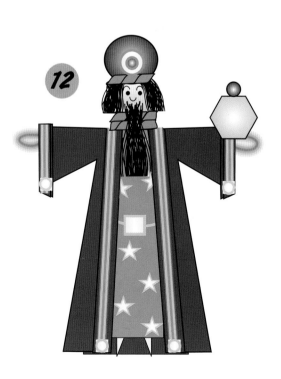

Camel

YOU WILL NEED:

1 ½ brown fuzzy sticks

1 small brown pompom

1 medium brown pompom

1 large brown pompom

Scrap of felt

String

Scissors

PVA glue

1 Cut the full length fuzzy stick in half. Take one of the three halves and bend over one end. Then bend it 3 cm along and fold it back on itself. Twist the fuzzy stick over and downwards at the centre to create a T shape.

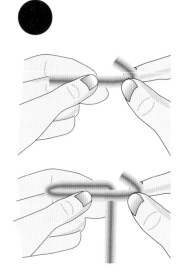

2 Bend the end back up towards the centre of the T. Glue the T shape to the medium pompom, then glue the small pompom on the front to finish the head.

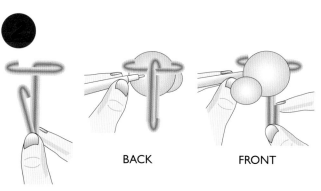

BACK   FRONT

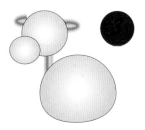

3 Glue the head to the large pompom.

4 Take the two remaining pieces of fuzzy stick, bend the ends over, then bend into a V shape. Each V makes two legs.

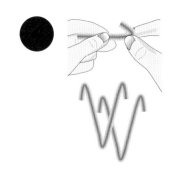

5 Take one set of legs and glue them under the large pompom facing backwards. Then glue the other legs facing forwards.

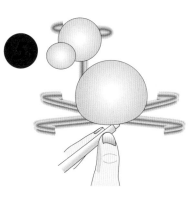

6 Cut a rectangular scrap of felt for a blanket and glue it over the camel's body. Tie a length of string around the camel's nose, to complete the model.

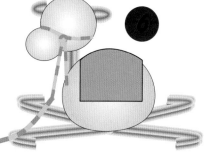

Angel

YOU WILL NEED:

Dolly peg

½ pink fuzzy stick

White felt, 9 x 18 cm

Cloak template (page 96)

Tracing paper and pencil

White paper

1 m yellow thread

1 m gold thread

1 ½ gold fuzzy sticks

Scissors

PVA glue

Black felt-tip pen

1 Take half a pink fuzzy stick. Bend over the ends to make the hands. Stick it to the back of the dolly peg to create the arms.

2 Take the yellow thread. Fold it in half and repeat until you have the desired length of hair, then glue it to the centre of the dolly peg's head.

3 For the gown, take the white felt and follow step 6 on page 64.

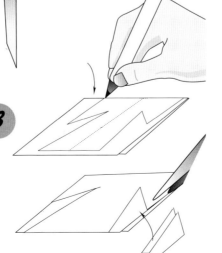

Top Tip
You will need to keep two of the left-over pieces cut from under the arm.

4 Keeping the gown in half, cut a small semicircle in the centre at the top, so when you unfold it you have a circle.

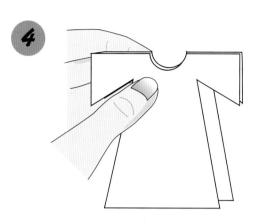

5 Gently place the gown over the angel's head, pulling out any hair trapped underneath. Glue the edges of the sides and sleeves together.

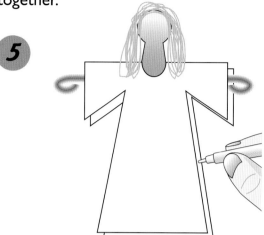

6 Using the two left-over pieces of felt, glue the straight edges onto the top of the gown, as shown.

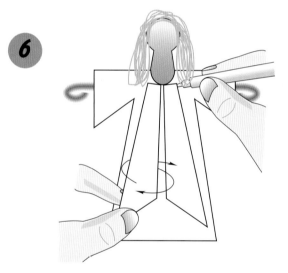

7 Pinch the loose ends and twist them over, so the longest points are now in the centre, and glue down.

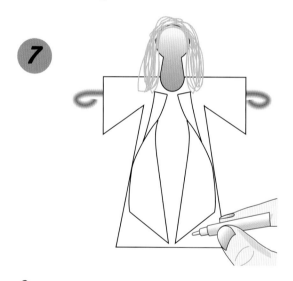

8 Trim the edges of the sleeves and the neck-line with gold thread.

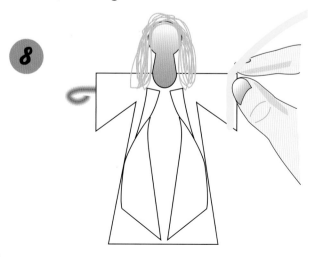

9 Finish the gown by gluing gold thread in a wavy pattern around the base.

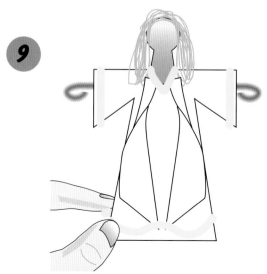

10 Take the half piece of gold fuzzy stick, bend it into a circle at one end and leave a stem to create the halo.

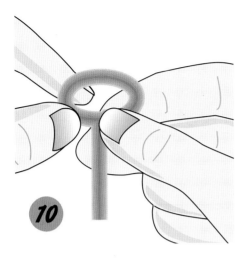

11 Using the full length of gold fuzzy stick, twist the two ends together to make a circle. Push the top and bottom in to make two big loops. Push the sides of the loops inwards to make the shape shown.

12 Glue the halo to the back of the head and the wings to the back of the gown. Snip the ends of the hair to make individual strands.

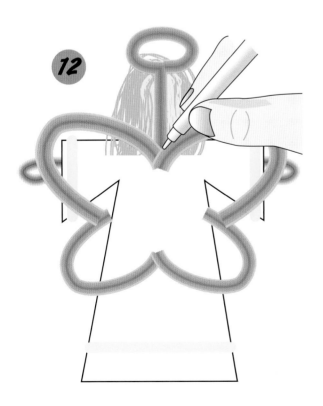

13 Use a black felt-tip pen to draw the angel's features. We have given ours a trumpet which you can make out of a left-over piece of fuzzy stick or a golf tee!

Stable

YOU WILL NEED:

Stable templates (pages **94** to **96**): stable front, stable back, stable sides **1** and **2**, beam, roof, stars **1** and **2**

Tracing paper and pencil

Cereal packet (flattened out)

Scissors

PVA glue

Coloured felt-tip pens, crayons or paints

1 Trace all the stable templates (listed right) onto the flattened-out cereal packet, then cut them out.

1

2 Ask an adult to cut out the windows and the slots. Then you can colour the pieces with crayons, felt-tip pens or paints.

2

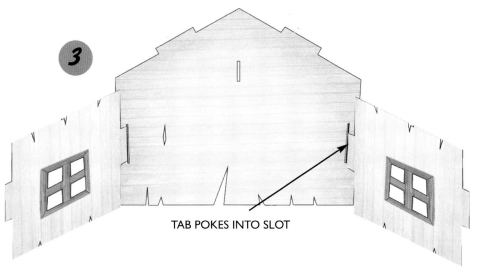

TAB POKES INTO SLOT

3 First, slot the two sides into the back of the stable.

4 Next, slot the beam into the back of the stable wall.

5 Attach the front of the stable by slotting it onto the side walls and the beam.

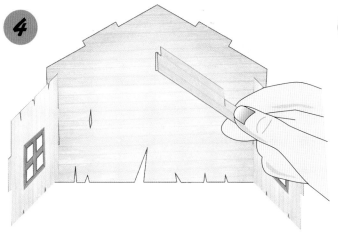

6 Bend the roof in the middle, as shown, then slot it onto the four tabs at the front and back of the stable.

7 To finish, slot the two star pieces together. Then push them into the cross in the centre of the roof.

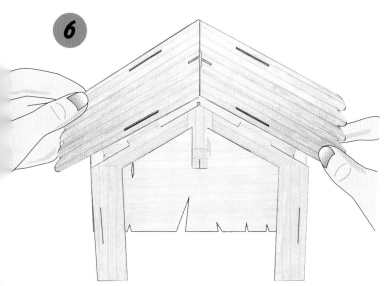

Knitted Baubles

You need to learn some basic knitting skills (pages 81 to 86) to make the gorgeous knitted bauble decorations on pages 87 to 93. These are advanced craft projects.

YOU WILL NEED:

Knitting needles

Wool in festive colours

2 half polystyrene balls per bauble, 43 mm diameter

Ribbon

Scissors

Fabric glue or PVA glue

Darning needle

Decorations: sequins, buttons, more ribbon

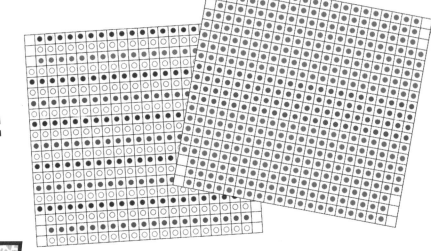

WARNING!
Take care when using knitting needles, darning needles and scissors as they have sharp points.

Using templates

Each project has a template for you to follow, including the stitches to use: knit stitch (a solid dot) and purl stitch (an unfilled dot). See pages 82 and 83. There's also a photograph of each finished bauble design, so you know what you're aiming for and the colours to use!

Casting On

The first step to mastering knitting is casting on – this means placing the required number of stitches onto a needle. Follow these simple instructions to start knitting!

1 Make a loop at the end of your wool.

2 Create a new loop in the wool and pull it through, as shown.

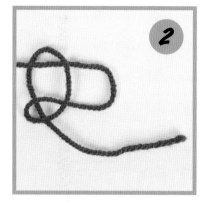

3 Carefully slip the end of one needle through the loop.

4 Pull both ends of the wool tightly to secure the knot on the needle.

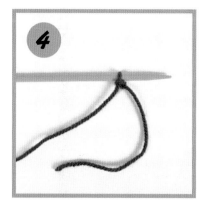

5 Wrap the wool over and around your thumb, as shown.

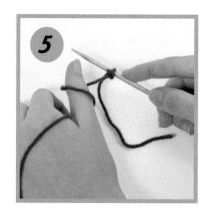

6 Place the needle through the wool.

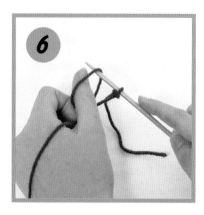

7 Pull the wool off your thumb and onto the needle. Pull to tighten.

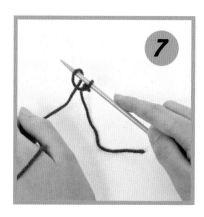

Knit Stitch

The knit stitch is one of two basic knitting stitches. When starting a new row, hold the needle with the stitches in your left hand. Knit from right to left, holding the yarn in your right hand.

1 Cast on the number of stitches you want (see page 81). Push the right-hand needle under the first stitch so the needles are crossed.

2 Wrap the wool around the right-hand needle anticlockwise (from back to front). It should lie between the two needles.

3 Insert the right-hand needle into the front of the left-hand loop, crossing the left-hand needle.

4 Pull the right-hand needle and loop off the left-hand needle. Pull the stitch tight. Repeat to complete a row.

Top Tip
When you have finished a row, count the stitches to make sure you haven't dropped any. Now begin to create your next row.

Purl Stitch

The purl stitch is another basic stitch, usually combined with the knit stitch. Try alternating a row of knit stitches with a row of purl stitches for a smooth surface, or experiment with other combinations of the two.

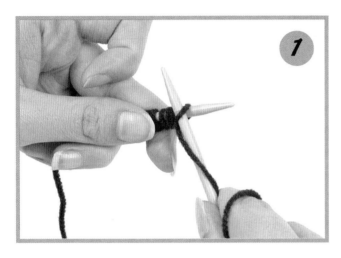

1 Cast on the number of stitches you want onto the left knitting needle.

2 Push the right-hand needle from right to left through the first stitch on the left needle. The right needle should be on top. Wrap the wool anticlockwise around the right needle.

3 Slide the right-hand needle down and to the back, so it catches the wool going down the middle of the loop. Slide the stitch on the left-hand needle off, transferring the stitch to the right.

4 When you have finished a row, count the stitches to make sure that you haven't dropped any. Now begin again to create your next row.

Increasing

Add an extra stitch to a row to increase the size of your knitting.

1 Knit one stitch as normal, but don't pull it off the left-hand needle.

2 Pull the right-hand needle behind the left-hand needle, as shown.

3 Push the right-hand needle into the back of the stitch on the other needle, as shown.

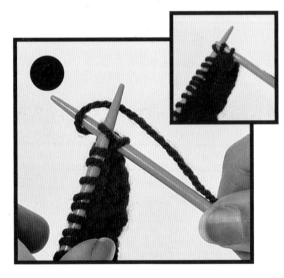

4 Wrap the wool anticlockwise around the right-hand needle. Knit the stitch as normal, pulling it off the other needle.

5 You should now have two stitches on your right-hand needle. Knit the rest of the row as normal. When you have one stitch on the left-hand needle, increase a stitch again.

Decreasing

Remove stitches from a row to decrease the size of your knitting.

To make your knitting narrower, knit or purl as normal, but push the right-hand knitting needle through two stitches instead of one at the start or the end of the row. The more rows you do this on, the quicker your knitting will shrink!

Dropped Stitch

If you spot a hole in your work, you have probably dropped a stitch.

Work up to the end of the row. Carefully slide the needle out of the stitches. Gently pull the wool to unravel the stitches until you have unravelled the row with the dropped stitch, then stop.

Carefully push the needle back through the stitches. The loose end of the wool needs to be at the pointed end of the needle. Count the stitches to make sure you have caught them all. Carry on knitting!

Casting Off

Casting off is the final step in the knitting process.

1 When you have finished knitting, you'll need to secure the final row to stop the wool unravelling. Hold the knitting on the left, as usual. Take the right-hand knitting needle and knit two stitches.

2 Push the tip of the left-hand needle through the front of the first stitch that you knitted on the right-hand needle.

3 Using the left needle, pull the first stitch on the right needle over the top of the second stitch on the right needle, so that it drops off. One stitch is now cast off!

4 Knit another stitch from the left needle onto the right needle. Repeat steps 2 and 3 until all the stitches but one are cast off.

5 Loosen the last stitch and pull out the needle, as shown.

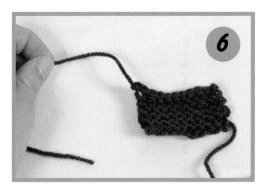

6 Cut the wool off the ball, leaving about 10 cm. Thread the end back through the loop, pull to tighten and tie a knot to secure it.

Ruby Glow

Learn how to make this ruby-red bauble on the next three pages.

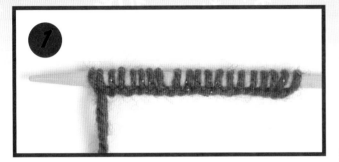

1 Following the diagram below, start by casting on 20 stitches.

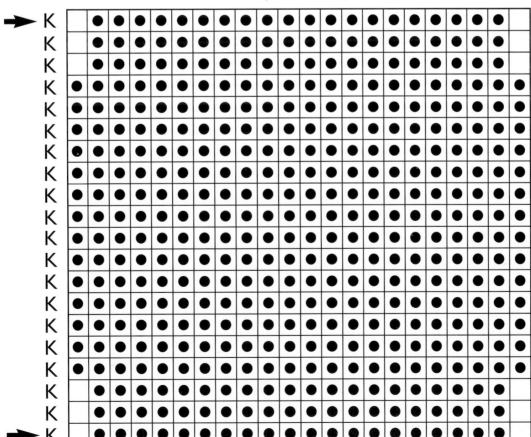

● K = Knit stitch

Cast on																					Top of knitting

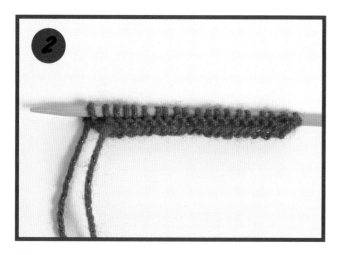

2 Knit another 2 rows of 20 stitches.

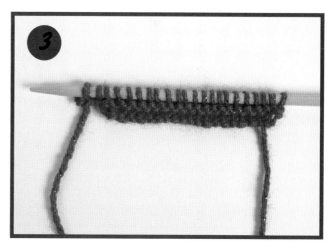

3 In row 4, expand your knitting by one extra stitch at each end.

4 Knit another 13 rows of 22 stitches.

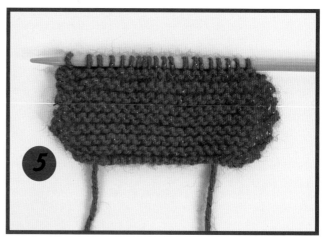

5 In row 18, decrease your knitting by a stitch at either end so you have 20 stitches on your needle again. Knit one more row.

6 In the final row, cast off (see page 86).

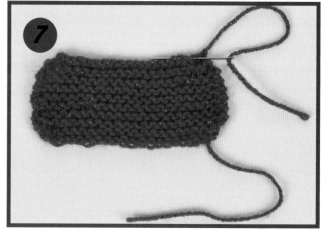

7 Thread the first loose end of the wool onto a darning needle. Thread the needle through the first row of stitches. Thread the last loose end of the wool onto a darning needle. Thread the needle through the last row of stitches.

8 Using a separate piece of wool, sew up the edges of the knitting to form a 'tube'. Don't trim the ends of the wool as you'll need them to gather up the top and bottom of the knitting later. Tuck the loose ends inside.

9 Pull the top loose thread tightly to gather the knitting up. Secure the end of the wool so it doesn't come undone.

10 Glue two polystyrene halves together to form a solid ball, then cut the hanging ribbon to about 14 cm in length and glue to the ball, as shown.

11 Gently push the polystyrene ball into the knitted tube.

12 Gather up the top of the knitting, as you did for the bottom. Make sure your ribbon is on the outside, ready for hanging.

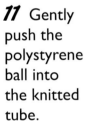

13 To decorate, glue a piece of lace around the centre of the bauble. Add a silver bow at the top. Your bauble is now complete!

Winter Wonder

Use multicoloured wool for colour variations on your bauble.

To decorate, use gold ribbon to tie a bow at the base of the hanging ribbon. At the centre of the bow, use buttons to decorate.

- ● K = Knit stitch
- ○ P = Purl stitch

Cast on   Top of knitting

→ K		●	●	●	●	●	●	●	●	●	●	●	●	●	●	●	●	●	●	●	●		
P		○	○	○	○	○	○	○	○	○	○	○	○	○	○	○	○	○	○	○	○		
K		●	●	●	●	●	●	●	●	●	●	●	●	●	●	●	●	●	●	●	●		
P	○	○	○	○	○	○	○	○	○	○	○	○	○	○	○	○	○	○	○	○	○	○	○
K	●	●	●	●	●	●	●	●	●	●	●	●	●	●	●	●	●	●	●	●	●	●	●
P	○	○	○	○	○	○	○	○	○	○	○	○	○	○	○	○	○	○	○	○	○	○	○
K	●	●	●	●	●	●	●	●	●	●	●	●	●	●	●	●	●	●	●	●	●	●	●
P	○	○	○	○	○	○	○	○	○	○	○	○	○	○	○	○	○	○	○	○	○	○	○
K	●	●	●	●	●	●	●	●	●	●	●	●	●	●	●	●	●	●	●	●	●	●	●
P	○	○	○	○	○	○	○	○	○	○	○	○	○	○	○	○	○	○	○	○	○	○	○
K	●	●	●	●	●	●	●	●	●	●	●	●	●	●	●	●	●	●	●	●	●	●	●
P	○	○	○	○	○	○	○	○	○	○	○	○	○	○	○	○	○	○	○	○	○	○	○
K	●	●	●	●	●	●	●	●	●	●	●	●	●	●	●	●	●	●	●	●	●	●	●
P	○	○	○	○	○	○	○	○	○	○	○	○	○	○	○	○	○	○	○	○	○	○	○
K	●	●	●	●	●	●	●	●	●	●	●	●	●	●	●	●	●	●	●	●	●	●	●
P	○	○	○	○	○	○	○	○	○	○	○	○	○	○	○	○	○	○	○	○	○	○	○
K	●	●	●	●	●	●	●	●	●	●	●	●	●	●	●	●	●	●	●	●	●	●	●
→ P	○	○	○	○	○	○	○	○	○	○	○	○	○	○	○	○	○	○	○	○	○	○	○

Cast off   Bottom of knitting

Razzle Dazzle

Try knitting with two different colours (strands) of wool at the same time for a mottled effect.

Use thinner wools, or the knitting will be too chunky for the polystyrene ball. Finish with a thin ribbon threaded with sparkly beads, as shown.

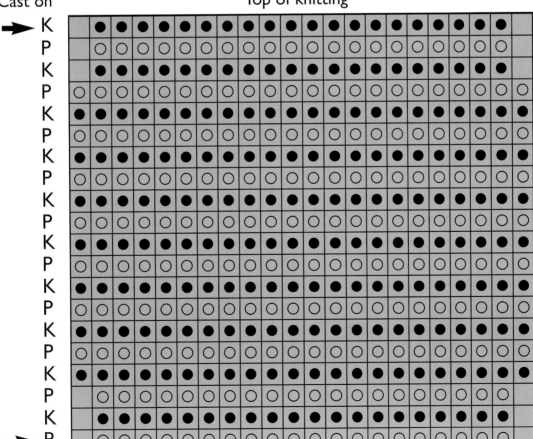

- ● K = Knit stitch
- ○ P = Purl stitch

Cast on   Top of knitting

→ K
   P
   K
   P
   K
   P
   K
   P
   K
   P
   K
   P
   K
   P
   K
   P
   K
→ P

Cast off   Bottom of knitting

ADULT HELP NEEDED

Festive Fancy

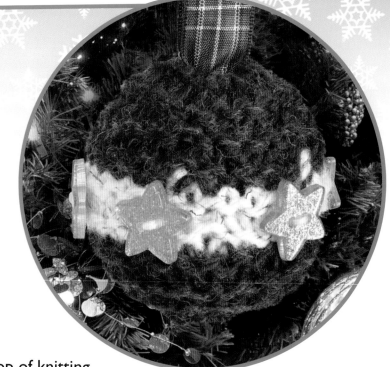

Sew gold buttons around the centre of the bauble. Try to find glittery buttons for extra festive sparkle!

Knit the first 8 rows with green and red wool mixed together. Then switch to white wool for 4 rows. Then switch back to green and red mixed together for the rest of the knitting.

● K = Knit stitch

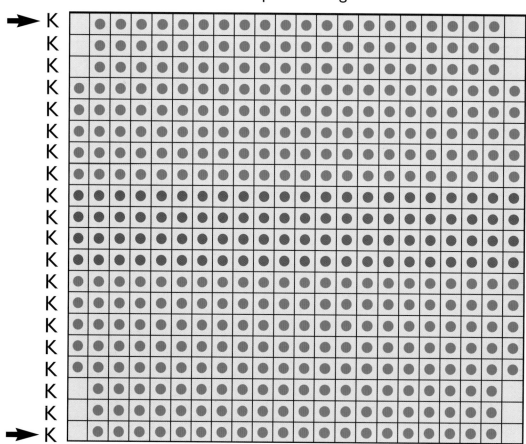

Cast on   Top of knitting

→ K
K
K
K
K
K
K
K
K
K
K
K
K
K
K
K
K
K
K
→ K

Cast off   Bottom of knitting

Evergreen

ADULT HELP NEEDED

To finish, use a lace hanging ribbon and decorate with a big chequered bow to match your bauble's colour.

- ● K = Knit stitch
- ○ P = Purl stitch

Cast on

Top of knitting

→ K
P
K
K
P
K
P
K
K
P
K
P
K
K
P
K
P
K
K
→ P

Cast off

Bottom of knitting

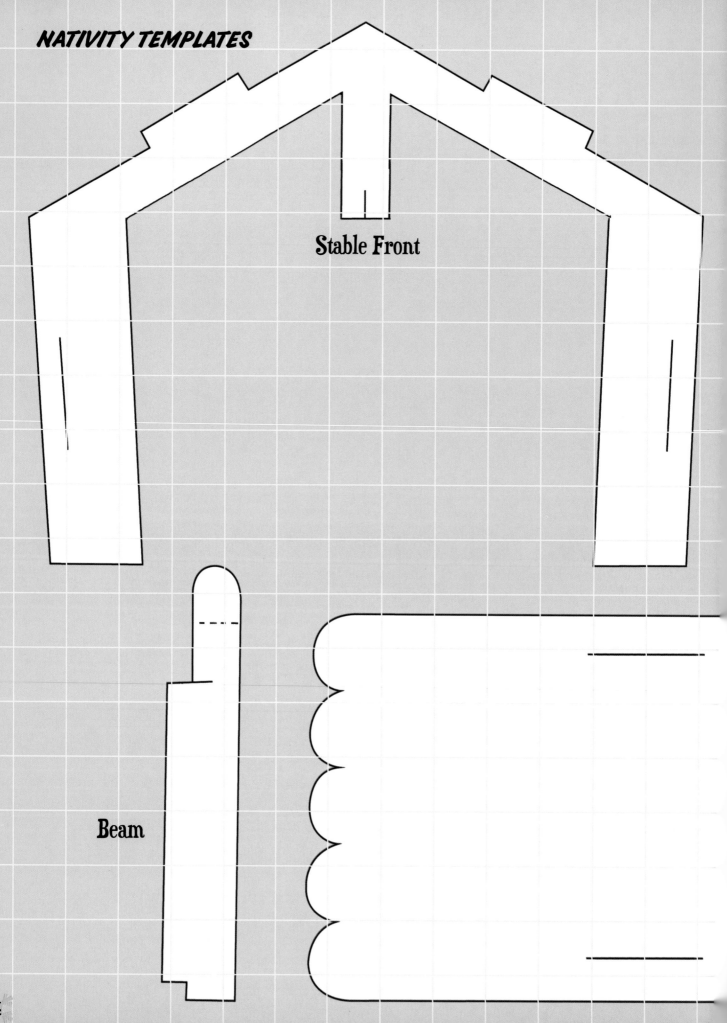

Stable Front

Beam

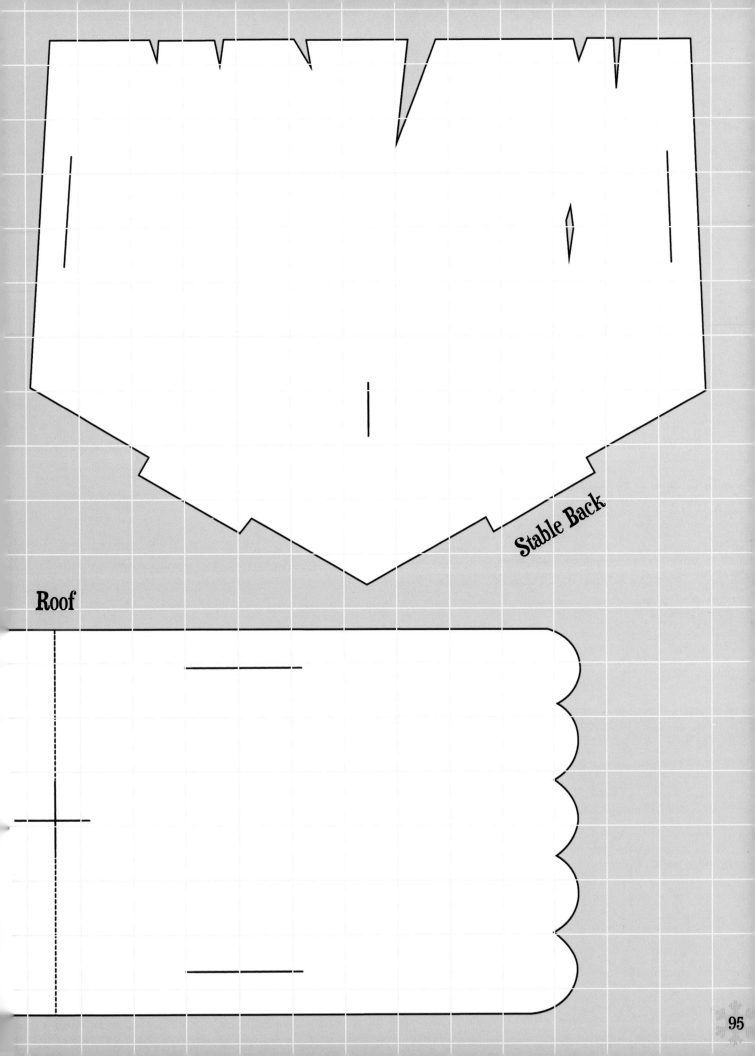

Stable Back

Roof

Cloak

Stable Side 1

Crib

Stable Side 2

Star 1

Star 2